Notes On My Life

(A simple do-it-yourself personal history)

Chris Fairweather

Published by Berhampore Press

Wellington, New Zealand.

All rights reserved

Copyright 2017

BerhamporePress@gmail.com

ISBN-13: 978-1547013708
ISBN-10: 1547013702

Table of Contents

Introduction 1

You and Your Parents 2

    Biographical information about you: 2

    Biographical information about your mother: 2

    Biographical information about your father: 2

Your Maternal Grandparents (mother's side of family) 3

    Biographical information about your grandfather: 3

    Biographical information about your grandmother: 3

Your Paternal Grandparents (father's side of family) 4

    Biographical information about your grandfather: 4

    Biographical information about your grandmother: 4

Places You Lived 5

Important Dates — Deaths, Births and Marriages 8

Significant People In My Life 11

Pets 15

Education 17

Higher Education 18

    Classes taken, skills gained, degrees completed, and other qualifications and learning: 18

Childhood Memories 19

    Memories from my early years: 19

    Memories from my middle years: 20

    Memories from high school: 21

    Memorable holiday/s: 22

Places I've Worked 23

Turning Points 27

Causes and Charities I've Supported 29

Musical Influences	31
A Typical Day	33
My Travels	35
Military Service	37
Family Traditions	39
Photographs	41
Hobbies and Interests	43
Cars, Bikes and Boats	45
Games I Enjoyed	46
Family Heirlooms and Their History	47
Famous People I Have Met	49
Memorable Events I've Attended	51
Inventions Made During My Life	53
A Story About When I was Naughty	55
A Time I Was Proud of Myself	57
A Story About My Mother	59
A Story About My Father	61
A Story About My Sibling/s	63
Notes About Other Significant Relatives	65
A Favorite Joke or Funny Story	67
The Best of Friends	69
My Morals and Values	73
My Politics	75
Medical History	77
An Interesting Medical Story	78
Philosophy of Life	79
Other Important Biographical or Historical Information	81

Introduction

Each life is unique. Use this book's simple framework to record your personal story. There are sections for you to record family traditions, important events you've attended, childhood memories, people who've influenced you, friends you've made over your lifetime, and all the shenanigans you've been involved in. Here you can record births, deaths and marriages, as well as your educational achievements, pets you've owned, and much, much more.

Eventually, this book can be passed down to your children where the information it contains will add to your family's rich history.

I often hear people say that they wish they'd known more about their parent's lives. It's a sad fact, but stories and traditions tend to get lost over time if they aren't archived. Don't let your part in your family's history fade into obscurity. Complete this book now. The generations to come will thank you for it.

Chris Fairweather

You and Your Parents

Biographical information about you:

First Name:

Middle Name/s:

Last Name: Nee:

Place of Birth: Date of Birth (DOB):

Sibling's Name/s and DOB:

Biographical information about your mother:

Mother's Name:

Middle Name/s:

Last Name: Nee:

Place of Birth: Date of Birth:

Sibling's Name/s and DOB:

Biographical information about your father:

Father's Name:

Middle Name/s:

Last Name:

Place of Birth: Date of Birth:

Sibling's Name/s and DOB:

Your Maternal Grandparents (mother's side of family)

Biographical information about your grandfather:

Grandfather's name:

Middle Name/s:

Last Name:

Place of Birth:

Date of Birth:

His father's Name:

His mother's Name:

His sibling's Name/s:

Biographical information about your grandmother:

Grandmother's Name:

Middle Name/s:

Last Name:					Nee:

Place of Birth:					Date of Birth:

Her father's Name:

Her mother's Name:

Her sibling's Name/s:

Your Paternal Grandparents (father's side of family)

Biographical information about your grandfather:

Grandfather's name:

Middle Name/s:

Last Name:

Place of Birth: Date of Birth:

His father's Name:

His mother's Name:

His sibling's Name/s:

Biographical information about your grandmother:

Grandmother's Name:

Middle Name/s:

Last Name: Nee:

Place of Birth: Date of Birth:

Her father's Name:

Her mother's Name:

Her sibling's Name/s:

Places You Lived

Address:

Number of Years: From: To:

Memory from this location:

Address:

Number of Years: From: To:

Memory from this location:

Address:

Number of Years: From: To:

Memory from this location:

Address:

Number of Years: From: To:

Memory from this location:

Address:

Number of Years: From: To:

Memory from this location:

Address:

Number of Years:					From:						To:

Memory from this location:

Address:

Number of Years:					From:						To:

Memory from this location:

Address:

Number of Years:					From:						To:

Memory from this location:

Address:

Number of Years:					From:						To:

Memory from this location:

Address:

Number of Years:					From:						To:

Memory from this location:

Address:

Number of Years:					From:						To:

Memory from this location:

Address:

Number of Years: From: To:

Memory from this location:

Address:

Number of Years: From: To:

Memory from this location:

Address:

Number of Years: From: To:

Memory from this location:

Address:

Number of Years: From: To:

Memory from this location:

Address:

Number of Years: From: To:

Memory from this location:

Address:

Number of Years: From: To:

Memory from this location:

Important Dates — Deaths, Births and Marriages

Date:

Event:

Date:

Event:

Date:

Event:

Date:

Event:

Date:

Event:

Date:

Event:

Date:

Event:

Date:

Event:

Date:

Event:

Date:

Event:

Date:

Event:

Date:

Event:

Date:

Event:

Date:

Event:

Date:

Event:

Date:

Event:

Date:

Event:

Date:

Event:

Date:

Event:

Date:

Event:

Date:

Event:

Date:

Event:

Date:

Event:

Date:

Event:

Date:

Event:

Date:

Event:

Significant People In My Life

A place to acknowledge the people who've made a significant impact on your life and why.

Pets

A place to list your pets, funny stories about them, and the impact they had on your life.

Education

Schools, memories, and friends made:

Year 1:

Year 2:

Year 3:

Year 4:

Year 5:

Year 6:

Year 7:

Year 8:

Year 9:

Year 10:

Year 11:

Year 12:

Higher Education

Classes taken, skills gained, degrees completed, and other qualifications and learning:

Childhood Memories

Memories from my early years:

Memories from my middle years:

Memories from high school:

Memorable holiday/s:

Places I've Worked

Employer:

Approx dates:

Memories & People:

Employer:

Approx dates:

Memories & People:

Employer:

Approx dates:

Memories & People:

Employer:

Approx dates:

Memories & People:

Employer:

Approx dates:

Memories & People:

Employer:

Approx dates:

Memories & People:

Employer:

Approx dates:

Memories & People:

Employer:

Approx dates:

Memories & People:

Employer:

Approx dates:

Memories & People:

Employer:

Approx dates:

Memories & People:

Employer:

Approx dates:

Memories & People:

Employer:

Approx dates:

Memories & People:

Turning Points

A place to note the significant events in your life that took you in a new direction or made you see the world differently.

Causes and Charities I've Supported

30

Musical Influences

A place to list the music you've enjoyed, your favorite groups, instruments you've played, concerts you've seen, and other music related memories.

A Typical Day

Tell us about a typical day. Life is not always charged with excitement. It is also about the routine

My Travels

List the exciting places you've been, the people you've met, what you've enjoyed, and the impact it's had on your life.

Military Service

I.D. or service number:

Details of service:

Family Traditions

Cultural traditions:

Holiday traditions:

Cooking traditions:

Other traditions:

Photographs

If you have printed photos, it pays to write the names and location on the back of the photo. For digital photos, you can put that information into the file name or make separate folders with those details on them. If you have any specific notes about photos you've got, or specific people you'd like to be in charge of archiving them, you can note that below.

Hobbies and Interests

A place to list your various interests, who first got you involved in that particular interest, and the impact it's had on your life.

Cars, Bikes and Boats

Everyone remembers their first car, or some journey they had. What were your experiences?

Games I Enjoyed

1.

2.

3.

4.

5.

More about your favorite game/s:

Family Heirlooms and Their History

Heirloom:

Where it came from:

___

Heirloom:

Where it came from:

___

Heirloom:

Where it came from:

___

Heirloom:

Where it came from:

___

Heirloom:

Where it came from:

___

Heirloom:

Where it came from:

___

Heirloom:

Where it came from:

___

Heirloom:

Where it came from:

___

Heirloom:

Where it came from:

_____

Heirloom:

Where it came from:

_____

Heirloom:

Where it came from:

_____

Heirloom:

Where it came from:

_____

Heirloom:

Where it came from:

_____

Heirloom:

Where it came from:

_____

Heirloom:

Where it came from:

_____

Heirloom:

Where it came from:

_____

Famous People I Have Met

Name:

Location:

Occasion:

Name:

Location:

Occasion:

Name:

Location:

Occasion:

Name:

Location:

Occasion:

Name:

Location:

Occasion:

Name:

Location:

Occasion:

Name:

Location:

Occasion:

Name:

Location:

Occasion:

Name:

Location:

Occasion:

Name:

Location:

Occasion:

Name:

Location:

Occasion:

Name:

Location:

Occasion:

Memorable Events I've Attended

Date:

Event:

Memories of event:

Date:

Event:

Memories of event:

Date:

Event:

Memories of event:

Date:

Event:

Memories of event:

Date:

Event:

Memories of event:

Date:

Event:

Memories of event:

Date:

Event:

Memories of event:

Date:

Event:

Memories of event:

Inventions Made During My Life

A place to note advances in technology, favorite inventions, and innovations that had a major impact on your life and why.

A Story About When I was Naughty

Nobody is 100% good, so share a time where you've been bad. It could be a funny story, or possibly a story of caution or regret.

A Time I Was Proud of Myself

Go on, don't be shy. Tell us about a time you were brave, achieved something important, or affected someone else's life in some significant way.

A Story About My Mother

A place to describe your mother's influence in your life and the things that made her who she was.

A Story About My Father

A place to describe your father's influence in your life and the things that made him who he was.

A Story About My Sibling/s

A memory about a brother or sister, or how a sibling had an influence on your life.

Notes About Other Significant Relatives

In this section, you might mention aunts, uncles, cousins, or any other relative that played an important part in your life.

A Favorite Joke or Funny Story

The Best of Friends

Friend's name:

Where you met:

Approx year:

Most vivid memory:

Friend's name:

Where you met:

Approx year:

Most vivid memory:

Friend's name:

Where you met:

Approx year:

Most vivid memory:

Friend's name:

Where you met:

Approx year:

Most vivid memory:

Friend's name:

Where you met:

Approx year:

Most vivid memory:

Friend's name:

Where you met:

Approx year:

Most vivid memory:

Friend's name:

Where you met:

Approx year:

Most vivid memory:

Friend's name:

Where you met:

Approx year:

Most vivid memory:

Friend's name:

Where you met:

Approx year:

Most vivid memory:

Friend's name:

Where you met:

Approx year:

Most vivid memory:

Friend's name:

Where you met:

Approx year:

Most vivid memory:

Friend's name:

Where you met:

Approx year:

Most vivid memory:

My Morals and Values

This is the place to mention any strong moral convictions or beliefs you have. How these have affected your life, and what you hope you've passed onto the next generation.

My Politics

A place to mention political influences or involvement, politicians you've liked or disliked and issues that have been important to you and why.

Medical History

Your medical history can be valuable to the generations that follow as many diseases have a genetic component. Early testing for some conditions can make a big difference to the outcome.

Conditions/Diseases to watch out for:

1.

2.

3.

4.

5.

6.

7.

An Interesting Medical Story

This could be about a childhood illness, or a major health scare. It can be funny, sad, about you, or about someone you love.

Philosophy of Life

A section for you to mention your basic beliefs, and how you feel about the big issues that face us all. This is also a good place to pass on a few words of wisdom to future generations.

80

Other Important Biographical or Historical Information

Every life is unique so there are bound to be things that are important to you that have been left out of this book. Don't hesitate to put those things here. In the case of family history, more is better. Who knows what will spark someone's interest in the future.

Made in the USA
Columbia, SC
26 November 2017